A Manatee Calf Grows Up

by Katie Marsico

Children's Press®
A Division of Scholastic Inc.
New York Toronto London Auckland Sydney
Mexico City New Delhi Hong Kong
Danbury, Connecticut

These content vocabulary word builders are for grades 1–2.

Subject Consultant: Susan H. Gray, MS, Zoology

Reading Consultant: Cecilia Minden-Cupp, PhD, Former Director of the Language and Literacy Program, Harvard Graduate School of Education, Cambridge, Massachusetts

Photographs © 2007: Brandon Cole Marine Photography: cover center inset, cover right inset, cover background, 1, 2, 4 bottom right, 13, 17, 20 bottom, 20 top right, 21 top right, 21 top left, 23 bottom right; Dembinsky Photo Assoc.: 6 left (Larime Photo), back cover, 9, 21 bottom (Mark J. Thomas); John Toebe: 4 bottom left, 8, 20 top left; Minden Pictures: 5 top left, 6 right (Heidi & Hans-Jurgen Koch), 23 bottom left (Norbert Wu); Nature Picture Library Ltd./Doug Perrine: 19; Photo Researchers, NY: cover left inset, 4 top, 11, 15, 20 center, 21 center (Douglas Faulkner), 5 bottom left, 14 (Alexis Rosenfeld); Seapics.com/Doug Perrine: 5 bottom right, 5 top right, 7, 10; Visuals Unlimited: 23 top left (Brandon Cole), 23 top right (Tom Walker).

Book Design: Simonsays Design!
Book Production: The Design Lab

Library of Congress Cataloging-in-Publication Data
Marsico, Katie, 1980–
A manatee calf grows up / by Katie Marsico.
    p. cm. — (Scholastic news nonfiction readers)
Includes bibliographical references.
ISBN-13: 978-0-531-17479-1
ISBN-10: 0-531-17479-4
1. Manatees—Growth—Juvenile literature. 2. Manatees—Development—
    Juvenile literature. I. Title. II. Series.
QL737.S63M363 2007
599.55—dc22   2006023796

1 2 3 4 5 6 7 8 9 10 R 16 15 14 13 12 11 10 09 08 07

CONTENTS

WORD HUNT

Look for these words as you read. They will be in **bold**.

calf
(caff)

newborn
(**nu**-born)

nursing
(**nurs**-ing)

mammals
(mam-uhlz)

manatee
(man-uh-tee)

sea grass
(see gras)

surface
(sur-fuhss)

Manatee Calves!

Splash! What's peeking out of the water? It's a baby **manatee**! A baby manatee is called a **calf**.

Manatees are **mammals**. Female mammals make milk in their bodies to feed their babies.

mammals

Manatees are large mammals that live in the ocean.

Manatees usually have just one baby at a time. A baby manatee is born underwater.

A manatee **newborn** weighs between 60 and 70 pounds (27 and 32 kilograms). That's about as much as an eight-year-old child!

newborn

Female manatees are called cows. Male manatees are called bulls.

What is one of the first things a newborn calf does?

Manatees must swim to the **surface** of the water to get air. A calf knows to do this right away.

surface

A manatee swims to the surface to get air.

A mother manatee always stays close to her calf. Mother and calf usually swim right next to each other.

How does a manatee feed her calf? A mother manatee feeds her calf milk from her body for about a year. This is called **nursing**.

A calf begins drinking its mother's milk a few hours after it is born.

The calf also starts to eat water plants when it is a few weeks old. **Sea grass** is a favorite food of manatees.

Manatee calves are born with teeth, so chewing plants is no problem.

sea grass

A manatee cow teaches her calf which plants are safe to eat.

Manatees live in warm water. A mother manatee shows her calf how to find warmer areas.

A manatee calf stays with its mother for about two years. It has a lot to learn!

Some calves live near their mothers even after they are two years old.

A female calf becomes an adult manatee when it is five years old.

Male calves become adults when they are nine years old.

It won't be long before the new adults have calves of their own!

A group of manatees gathers in warm water in Florida.

A MANATEE CALF GROWS UP!

1 A female manatee gives birth to her baby underwater.

newborn

2 The newborn calf swims to the surface of the water to breathe air.

3 A few hours after the calf is born, it begins to nurse from its mother.

20

7 A female calf becomes an adult manatee when it is five years old. A male calf becomes an adult at nine years old.

6 Until it is two years old, the calf stays with its mother. The calf learns how to find food and warm water.

5 Hungry manatee calves begin eating plants when they are only a few weeks old.

4 The mother manatee and her calf usually swim right next to each other.

YOUR NEW WORDS

calf (caff) a baby animal such as a manatee, cow, elephant, or whale

mammals (**mam**-uhlz) animals that nurse their babies

manatee (**man**-uh-tee) a kind of mammal that lives in the ocean

newborn (**nu**-born) a person or animal that was just born

nursing (**nurs**-ing) feeding a baby milk from its mother's body

sea grass (see gras) grasslike plants that grow in the waters along a seacoast

surface (**sur**-fuhss) the outside or outer face of something, such as a body of water

THESE ANIMALS ARE WATER MAMMALS, TOO!

dolphin

sea lion

seal

whale

INDEX

FIND OUT MORE

Book:

Martin-James, Kathleen. *Gentle Manatees*. Minneapolis: Lerner Publications, 2005.

Website:

National Geographic Kids: Creature Feature—Manatees
http://www.nationalgeographic.com/kids/creature_feature/0307/manatees.html

MEET THE AUTHOR

Katie Marsico lives with her family outside of Chicago, Illinois. She often visits Florida's Gulf Coast and always has her eye out for manatees that might be swimming by!